D1289599

IS THERE LIFE OUT THERE?

THE LIKELIHOOD OF ALIEN LIFE AND WHAT IT WOULD LOOK LIKE

CAROL HAND

ROSEN
PUBLISHING

NEW YORK

Published in 2016 by The Rosen Publishing Group, Inc.
29 East 21st Street, New York, NY 10010

Copyright © 2016 by The Rosen Publishing Group, Inc.

First Edition

Library of Congress Cataloging-in-Publication Data

Hand, Carol, 1945- author.
Is there life out there? : the likelihood of alien life and what it would look like / Carol Hand. — First edition.
    pages cm. — (The search for other Earths)
Includes bibliographical references and index.
ISBN 978-1-4994-6294-4 (library bound)
1. Life on other planets—Juvenile literature. 2. Life (Biology)—Juvenile literature. 3. Extrasolar planets—Juvenile literature. I. Title.
QB54.H287 2016
576.8'39—dc23
                                                                            2015022067

Manufactured in China

CONTENTS

People have always marveled at the sight of the night sky and wondered about its secrets. Here, two young amateur astronomers explore the skies using a reflector telescope.

WHY SEARCH FOR ALIEN LIFE?

The Institute of Physics says, "If you hold up a grain of sand, the patch of sky it covers contains 10,000 galaxies." According to *Sky & Telescope* magazine, astronomers estimate there may be 100 billion galaxies in the observable universe and 300 billion stars just in our own Milky Way galaxy. There may be roughly 70 billion trillion (7 followed by 22 zeroes, or 7×10^{22}) stars in the universe. Given this vastness of space, how could there not be life out there? With that multitude of stars, many (millions or even billions) must have planets, and many of those planets must have Earth-like conditions where life has formed and even created civilizations. But ideas about the existence of alien life are so far just guesses, or at best, estimates. No one really knows.

Why should we search for alien life? The most obvious reason is practical. All space exploration, including the search for extraterrestrial (alien) life, requires new technology. What begins in satellites ends up in items for everyday use. For example, miniaturized electronic components led to the tiny computer chips now powering (among other things) everyone's cell phones. It takes highly educated people to develop these new technologies, so space exploration energizes the field of education and produces skilled workers able to advance the economy.

But the idea of better jobs or better technology is not even on the radar of most exobiologists—the scientists who search for alien life. Curiosity, a thirst for understanding, and a sense of adventure drives these scientists. They don't just want to guess or believe in alien life—they want to know. Where do humanity and planet Earth fit into the universe? Where did humans come from, and where are we going? Are humans the only intelligent life, or even the only life, in the vastness of space? Or do we have galactic neighbors? Curiosity about these and other big questions has spurred progress throughout human history.

When Copernicus, in 1543, showed that Earth revolved around the sun, rather than the other way around, he shattered the centuries-old assumption that Earth was the center of the universe. People had to absorb the idea that the entire universe might not be designed around human life. The Copernican revolution profoundly changed the human worldview— how people thought about themselves and their place in the universe.

How will twenty-first-century humans react if we discover we are not alone in the universe? If some of those billions upon billions of stars are home to planets that nourish life or even civilizations? Will we cower on our home planet and ignore them? Will we arm ourselves and prepare to repel alien invasions or even try to get the aliens before they get us? Or will we enter a new era of humanity, where we learn, explore, and evolve as human beings and as citizens, not just of planet Earth, but of the universe?

CHAPTER ONE

WHAT ARE WE LOOKING FOR?

Everything that we know about life, we learned on Earth. We base our understanding of life on a sample size of one. Thus, it makes sense that scientists would base the search for alien life on what we know about Earth life. Surprisingly, though, we know relatively little about life on Earth. No biologist can even give a precise definition of life.

Over the centuries, scientists have figured out the basic rules of chemistry and physics. Space exploration has shown that certain "laws of nature" apply throughout the universe. For example, water is a chemical compound composed of two hydrogen atoms and one oxygen atom. This definition determines all characteristics of water and distinguishes it from all other chemicals. Water will be H_2O no matter where it occurs in the universe. But before scientists understood elements and how they combine to form compounds, they "defined" water by listing its characteristics—it is colorless, odorless, tasteless, and liquid at room temperature; it freezes at 32 degrees Fahrenheit (0°Celsius); it vaporizes at 212 degrees Fahrenheit (100°C); and so on. This list was long and useful, but it did not uniquely distinguish water from other

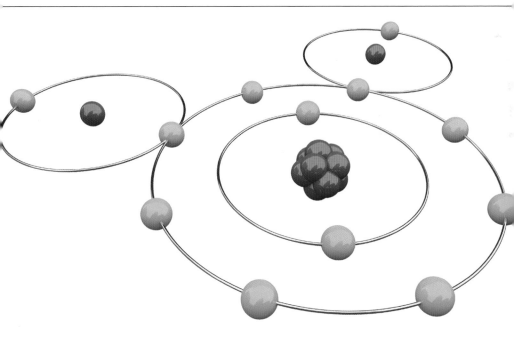

The chemical compound water is H_2O throughout the universe. This atomic diagram shows its single oxygen atom, two smaller hydrogen atoms, and the protons, neutrons, and electrons comprising each.

liquids, such as vinegar or alcohol. In the twenty-first century, scientists have similar problems as they try to precisely define life.

DEFINING EARTH LIFE

To investigate alien life, the National Aeronautics and Space Administration (NASA) developed a working definition of life: "Life is a self-sustaining chemical system capable of Darwinian evolution." But this definition is not precise. A human embryo is alive but not self-sustaining. A single organism is alive but, by itself, cannot undergo evolution, which only occurs in populations. Still, if scientists found a single alien object having the characteristics of Earth life, they would likely assume they had found alien life.

Like chemists of old, today's biologists define life by listing its important characteristics. A cell is the smallest structural unit considered alive; thus, all life is composed of one or more cells. Cells are made of organic, or carbon-based, molecules having a carbon backbone with other atoms attached. The six most abundant elements found in organic molecules are carbon, hydrogen, nitrogen, oxygen, phosphorus, and sulfur (often abbreviated "CHNOPS"). These elements combine to form four major types of "life compounds"— proteins, carbohydrates, fats or lipids, and nucleic acids. The organic compound that most identifies life is the nucleic acid DNA, the genetic material that contains instructions for present and future generations of life. Another key molecule is ATP, which provides energy for life processes.

Life processes are chemical reactions occurring within and among cells. The three essential life processes are metabolism, replication, and evolution. Life must constantly absorb energy (food) to survive. Metabolism is the process of chemically breaking down food and converting it to ATP energy. Life must continue itself. Replication is the process of copying genetic material (DNA) and passing it on to future generations by reproduction. Life must adapt to change. Evolution is genetic change, or

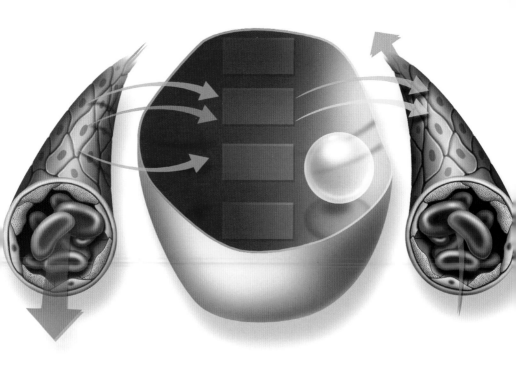

Every living cell undergoes metabolism, an essential life process. Food enters cells through blood vessels and is broken down to release energy and nutrients. Blood removes waste products.

adaptation of populations, in response to environmental stresses. Evolutionary changes occur in the DNA molecule, and the changes are passed on to new generations. Life characteristics such as movement, growth, and death follow naturally from these three essential processes.

EARTH LIFE IS DIVERSE

Most Earth life is not even visible but consists of microscopic, single-celled bacteria with very simple cells. These tiny cells contain few internal structures, and their DNA is not protected by a nucleus. In 1998, scientists at the University of Georgia estimated the total number of bacteria on Earth. Their estimate was 5 million trillion trillion (5 followed by 30 zeroes, or 5×10^{30}). For comparison, the U.S. Census Bureau's World Population Clock gave the human population in June 2015 as approximately 7.24 billion (or 7.24×10^{9}). Earth's diverse microscopic

THE CHANGING DEFINITION OF LIFE

Throughout human history, people's definitions of life have changed. In ancient times, people accepted the concept of vitalism. They thought organic, or living, material contained a nonphysical element called a "vital force" absent from inorganic, or nonliving, material. Later, mechanism became prevalent. This concept defined humans and other animals as "automata," or mechanical devices that differed from artificial structures only in their degree of complexity. For nearly three hundred years, people argued over these two concepts. Only in the mid-1800s, when early biologists discovered cells and microorganisms, did the concept of life widely accepted today begin to develop.

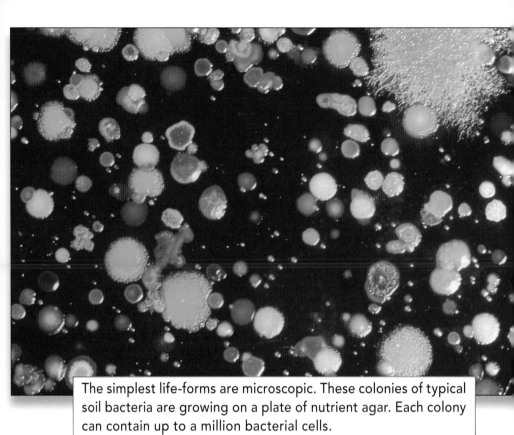

The simplest life-forms are microscopic. These colonies of typical soil bacteria are growing on a plate of nutrient agar. Each colony can contain up to a million bacterial cells.

life vastly outnumbers—and outweighs—its visible life. Bacteria exist 5 to 10 miles (8 to 16 kilometers) high in the atmosphere and 7 miles (11 km) below the surface, in the deepest part of the ocean.

Life more complex than bacteria has "true" cells, much larger than bacterial cells. They contain complex internal structures and enclose their DNA within a central nucleus. Organisms with true cells also show great diversity. Many, including protozoa and green algae, are single-celled. Others are many-celled and range in size from microscopic worms to redwood trees to blue whales. They also vary greatly in structure, behavior, methods of obtaining food, and habitats. Like bacteria, they occur nearly everywhere on Earth.

EXTREMOPHILES

Extremophiles are a special case of life on Earth. They thrive under conditions too extreme for most organisms to live. Scientists classify extremophiles by their type of extreme environment. Astrophysicist Sujan Sengupta explains that thermophiles live at hot temperatures of 140–176 °F (60–80°C) and hyperthermophiles live above 176°F (80°C). Other extremophiles can live under extreme conditions such as low temperature, high radiation, high pressure, low pressure, very acidic pH, very basic pH, extreme salinity, drought, or even starvation. Most (but not all) extremophiles are bacterialike. Some are adapted to two or more extreme conditions. According to C. Michael Hogan in *The*

Life can adapt to extreme conditions. Here, volcanic gases bubble up from geothermal vents on the ocean floor. These heated gases help extremophiles survive in the deepest ocean.

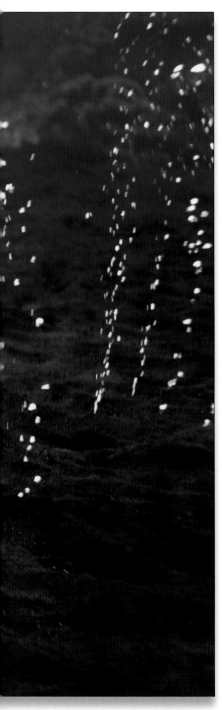

Encyclopedia of Earth, organisms living in thermal vents on the deep ocean floor are adapted to extreme pressure, temperatures exceeding 176°F (80°C), and high levels of sulfur and methane.

Earth's extreme environments help scientists understand which planets or moons might harbor Earth-like life. They can compare environmental conditions on those planets or moons (such as atmospheric gases, temperature, and pressure) with extremophile environments to determine if life could survive there. Seth Shostak, senior astronomer at the SETI

Institute (an organization that searches for alien life), says many planets might have conditions similar to those found deep in Earth's oceans, very cold regions such as Antarctica, or boiling regions such as hot springs. These planets could not support most Earth life, but they could theoretically support extremophiles.

LOOKING FOR BIOSIGNATURES

Vast distances mean scientists must search for alien life indirectly. They observe planets and moons in the solar system using Earth-based and space-based telescopes. They also send satellites or probes that fly by, orbit, or even land on moons or planets to collect data. Microbes are far too small to photograph, so scientists look for biosignatures—the presence of elements or compounds associated with life. Searching for life on exoplanets (planets orbiting stars outside our solar system) will be much more difficult, but researchers are developing strategies. Space-based telescopes equipped with spectrographs will look for biosignatures in

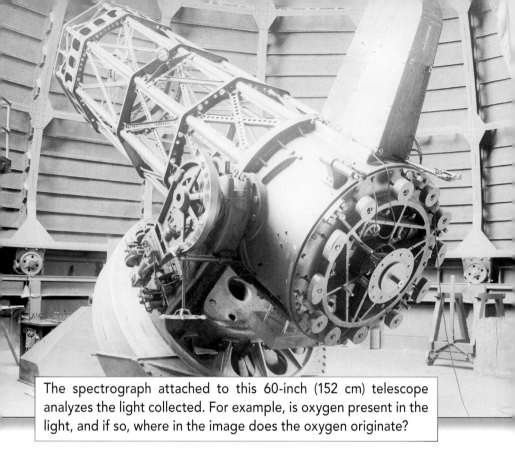

The spectrograph attached to this 60-inch (152 cm) telescope analyzes the light collected. For example, is oxygen present in the light, and if so, where in the image does the oxygen originate?

the planets' atmospheres. Spectrographs analyze light energy reflected by planets or stars. By reading this reflected light, scientists can determine elements and compounds present in the atmosphere. This indicates whether a planet might have life.

A key biosignature is water, which is necessary for all life on Earth. Another is oxygen. Oxygen is chemically reactive, so it is used up and must be constantly replenished in the atmosphere to be present in large quantities. On Earth, photosynthesis replenishes oxygen. High oxygen concentrations on an exoplanet would strongly indicate the presence of life, as would high concentrations of carbon-based chemicals, such as methane or carbon dioxide. Another possibility is chlorophyll, the green pigment that plants use in photosynthesis. Chlorophyll would be visible only if vegetation levels were very large and if the exoplanet had little cloud cover, leaving its surface visible.

The search for alien life is just beginning, and so far, it is based on what we know of Earth life. But as scientists increase their knowledge, they may discover new possibilities. Who knows what exotic life-forms might be out there?

CHAPTER TWO

WHERE ARE WE LOOKING?

Our solar system has eight planets with at least 146 moons. The five dwarf planets have six known moons. By mid-2015, the Kepler Space Telescope had discovered 1,918 exoplanets and 4,604 "Kepler candidates" not yet analyzed and confirmed as exoplanets. How do exobiologists decide where to look for life? Is every moon or planet equally likely? If not, what characteristics do they look for?

THE GOLDILOCKS ZONE

In the classic fairy tale, Goldilocks tasted two bowls of porridge before tasting a third, which was not too hot or too cold, but just right.

NASA's Kepler Space Telescope, launched in 2009, orbits the sun rather than Earth. This very stable orbit avoids problems including radiation, magnetism, and gravity associated with Earth orbits.

Exobiologists do exactly the same thing when considering possible sites for extraterrestrial life. They determine a planet's temperature and atmospheric pressure and calculate the distance from its star at which life could exist. Typical Earth life requires temperatures and pressures at which water can exist as a liquid. Water should neither boil away nor always remain frozen. The planet also requires an atmosphere that traps heat and keeps the surface warm (the greenhouse effect). Planets meeting these criteria are in what exobiologists call the Goldilocks Zone. The Goldilocks Zone is also called the habitable zone or life zone. These planets are candidates for where life might have evolved.

But Earth life exists in more places than we thought possible. Bacteria can live (among other places) in boiling water, oxygen-free conditions, or water three times as salty as the ocean. These findings suggest that life (at least bacterial life) might also exist on planets once thought uninhabitable. As scientists discover more extremophiles, the Goldilocks Zone keeps expanding.

The distance of the Goldilocks Zone from its star varies with the star's size and temperature. In our own solar system, Mercury is too hot. Venus is even hotter and has a dense, toxic atmosphere. Mars may be too cold. Earth lies in the Goldilocks Zone, approximately 93 million miles (149,668,992 km) from the sun. The

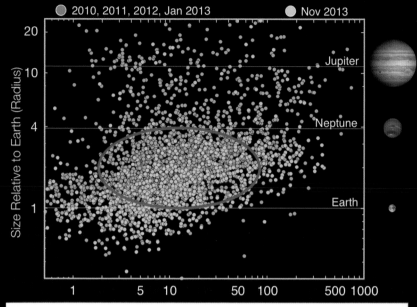

Most "planet candidates" discovered by Kepler range from Earth-to Neptune-sized (see oval). Neptune is about four times as large as Earth. Most have shorter orbital periods (years) than Earth.

Goldilocks Zone would be much closer to a red dwarf star, a type of star smaller and cooler than our yellow sun. For a giant, hot blue star, the Goldilocks Zone would be much farther away. Calculations suggest that most solar systems in the Milky Way may have one to three planets in their habitable zones. Scientists have not located potential "Goldilocks planets" for all stars with known exoplanets. Even if these planets exist, there is no guarantee that they will have liquid water, but the possibility exists.

SEEKING LIFE IN THE SOLAR SYSTEM

Our solar system has two types of planets—relatively small and rocky inner planets (Mercury, Venus, Earth, and Mars), and outer planets known as gas giants (Jupiter, Saturn, Uranus, and Neptune), each with many moons. The most likely places to find Earth-like life are small, rocky planets with moderate temperatures, water, and atmospheres. These conditions seem to rule out Mercury and Venus, as well as the gas giants. However, planetary scientist David Grinspoon thinks microbial life might float in Venus's upper atmosphere, where microbes could feed on sulfur dioxide and carbon monoxide.

In our solar system, Mars is the strongest possibility for life. Smaller and less dense than Earth, with only one-tenth of Earth's mass, Mars's atmosphere is similar to that of Venus (with 95 percent CO_2) but much less dense. It has polar caps similar to Earth's and seasons with strong temperature fluctuations. Summer at the equator reaches 32 F° (0°C) or more, and winter at the poles reaches -148 F° (-100°C). The Spirit and Opportunity rovers, which landed on Mars in 2004, sent back photographs of valleys and meandering streambeds apparently carved by water that once flowed on the planet's surface. In 2012, the *Curiosity* rover, carrying a suitcase-sized science lab, landed in the Gale Crater. Curiosity's lab determined that the crater once contained liquid water, which has since evaporated. In 2014, it found evidence of

The Rover Environmental Monitoring System (REMS) on the Mars Curiosity Rover has provided information on the air pressure, humidity, temperature, wind speed, and UV radiation on Mars.

methane gas, often produced by microbes, and of carbon-based molecules in sandstone rocks. These organic compounds suggest Mars has or once had microscopic life.

Some moons of Jupiter and Saturn might also have life. In 2005, the *Cassini* spacecraft photographed water geysers spouting from cracks in the frozen surface of Saturn's tiny moon Enceladus. Gravity between Enceladus and Saturn's other moons may be warming the water. Saturn's largest moon, Titan, is the only place in the solar system (other than Earth) with liquid lakes on its surface. But Titan's lakes are filled with ethane and methane (liquid natural gas), not water. Titan's active chemistry suggests extremophiles might live there. Ice 10 miles (16 km) thick covers Jupiter's moon Europa, but beneath the ice are huge oceans of salty water. Photosynthesis cannot occur in Europa's dark oceans, but geothermal heat, chemical synthesis, or organic compounds falling from above might have kindled life. Jupiter's moons Ganymede and Callisto may also have liquid oceans buried beneath about 60 miles (96 km) of solid rock.

SEEKING LIFE IN THE GALAXY

A team of Swiss astronomers discovered the first extrasolar planet, or exoplanet, in 1995. France launched the first mission dedicated to discovering exoplanets in 2006. NASA launched the first U.S. exoplanet mission, the Kepler Space Telescope, in 2009. Kepler's discoveries indicate most planets in the galaxy are probably small. It has found solar systems with multiple planets and very hot, low-density gas giants orbiting close to their stars (colloquially dubbed "Hot Jupiters"). Almost two thousand new planets had been discovered by 2015.

Astronomers find many exoplanets using the transit method. As the exoplanet transits, or moves in front of its star, the star dims, revealing the planet's presence. Transits also allow astronomers to determine a planet's size, the distance from its star, and the shape of its orbit—that is, whether it is circular or nearly so (like Earth) or more elliptical. This helps deduce the length of the planet's seasons and its rotation period. Spectroscopic analysis determines the color and amount of light reflected from a planet, which provides information about the density and composition of its atmosphere. For the few exoplanets studied, astronomers have detected a variety of biosignatures, including water (H_2O), as well as methane (CH_4), carbon monoxide (CO), and carbon dioxide (CO_2).

Minitab, a statistical software company, shows information on exoplanets graphi-

In December 2000, NASA's *Cassini* spacecraft captured two moons of Jupiter in this photograph. Europa is visible below and to the left of Jupiter's Great Red Spot. Callisto is at lower left.

cally, using the Earth Similarity Index (ESI), which compares an exoplanet's similarity to Earth. The ESI is based on estimates of exoplanet parameters including radius, density, and

EYEBALL PLANETS

Three-fourths of the galaxy's stars are cool red dwarfs, with between one-tenth and one-half the mass of the sun. Planets orbiting red dwarfs often have water, but they are tidally locked, with the same side of the planet (the daylight side) always facing the star. If the planet is cool enough, the daylight side has a huge, liquid ocean. On hotter planets, the ocean evaporates, resulting in a large land mass surrounded by water on the temperate, day-night boundary and huge ice sheets on the night side. On these so-called eyeball planets, the "pupil" of the "eyeball" faces the star. The boundary region forms a "ring of life"—the only place where life could exist

surface temperature. Values range from 0 to 1, with Earth's value being 1. The closer a planet's ESI is to 1, the more like Earth it is. For comparison, the ESI of Venus is 0.78, and the ESI of Mars is 0.64. According to Minitab, twenty-three exoplanets and exoplanet candidates have ESIs greater than 0.80, and five of these have values greater than 0.90. Eighteen of the twenty-three are superterrans. The twenty-three planets fall into two groups. Earth twins have similar stars, so they orbit at distances similar to Earth and

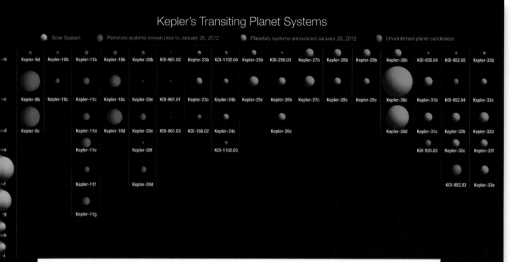

Kepler's Transiting Planet Systems

Solar System   Planetary systems known prior to January 26, 2012   Planetary systems announced January 26, 2012   Unconfirmed planet candidates

By January 2012, Kepler scientists had verified seventeen stars having multiple transiting planets. Given the tiny slice of space so far examined, many more planets likely remain to be discovered.

have years of approximately the same length as an Earth year. Earth cousins are very similar to Earth but orbit near small red dwarf stars and have years that are relatively very short. So far, astronomers have found no true Earth twins, but the search continues. The technology for analyzing exoplanets is still new in the history of space exploration and likely to advance rapidly in the coming years.

In July 2015, astronomers discovered a likely candidate for "Earth 2.0." An exoplanet called Kepler 452b orbits a star very similar to our sun every 385 days, making its year only slightly longer than Earth's 365-day year. This puts it

WHICH PLANETS ARE HABITABLE?

The Planet Habitability Laboratory (PHL) at the University of Puerto Rico at Arecibo has developed a Habitability Exoplanet Catalog (HEC), placing known exoplanets in three temperature categories—hot, warm, and cold—and six mass or size categories. Three of these eighteen categories have temperatures and masses suitable for supporting Earth-like life. All are in the warm zone; they include three size classes: subterran (0.1–0.5 times the mass of Earth, or M_E), terran (0.5–2 M_E), and superterran (2–10 M_E). As of 2014, there were no known planets in the warm subterran class, only one (Earth itself) in the warm terran class, and twenty in the warm superterran class. That is, so far, 1.1 percent of known exoplanets might be candidates for life.

squarely within the Goldilocks Zone, where liquid water may exist. Astronomers still aren't sure whether the planet is rocky or gaseous. At 1.6 times the size of Earth, it could be either. NASA astronomer Jon Jenkins, lead author of the paper describing the planet, says its chance of being rocky is 50 to 62 percent. If rocky, it would have about five times Earth's mass and double its gravity. It likely has a thick, cloudy

Kepler 186F was the first exoplanet validated to exist in the habitable zone of its star. Its discovery proved that Earth-sized planets existed in the habitable zones of other stars.

atmosphere and active volcanoes, and it has about 20 percent more sunlight than Earth. It is older than Earth, having spent nearly 6 (instead of 4.6) billion years in its habitable zone, so it has had longer to develop life. But 452b probably won't be on the short list for the first exoplanet we visit. It is 1,400 light-years from Earth, and there are probably at least sixty equally likely candidates for Earth 2.0 within thirty light-years that have not yet been discovered.

CHAPTER THREE

HOW LIKELY IS ALIEN LIFE?

Most people know the Nobel Prize–winning physicist Enrico Fermi as the builder of the first atomic bomb. But in 1950, in a lunchtime conversation with fellow scientists, Fermi asked a question that is still debated. The lunch crowd was discussing the probability that the universe contains many intelligent, even sophisticated societies. Most thought this was highly likely. But Fermi reasoned that, if such galactic societies exist, they have had plenty of time to explore and populate the galaxy, even considering huge interstellar distances and limits imposed by the speed of light. So Fermi asked the simple question, "Where is everybody?"

Enrico Fermi's classic experiments at the University of Chicago led to the first controlled nuclear reaction. He was also a leader on the Manhattan Project, which developed the first atomic bomb.

THE FERMI PARADOX

Scientists have offered many answers to Fermi's question, now known as the Fermi paradox. Some have dismissed the idea—there is no paradox, they say, because there are no extraterrestrials. Others suggest interstellar travel is too expensive, no good energy source exists, or aliens simply choose not to travel the galaxy. Or perhaps, before civilizations can colonize the galaxy, they collapse, destroy themselves, or run out of resources. Still others think the galaxy might be colonized (and might have sent visitors to

This photo, "Earthrise," was taken on Christmas Eve, 1968, from Earth's moon's orbit. The first view of Earth from space inspired humans to explore space and understand their place in it.

Earth), but humans just haven't noticed. Alien technology might be extremely advanced, so aliens could easily observe us without our knowledge. Some even support the Zoo Hypothesis—the idea that Earth might be an exhibit for alien tourists or sociologists.

In 1998, NASA scientist Geoffrey A. Landis proposed a "percolation theory" explaining how interstellar colonization might occur without humans encountering alien life. Landis assumed: 1) Interstellar travel is possible, although difficult, and the distance over which a colony can be established is limited; and 2) Each colony is far from its parent civilization and will eventually develop its own independent culture. Because of time, distance, and cost, some colonies will choose not to form new colonies. New colonies will form clusters, with each planet settling the planets nearest them—and only settling those with suitable living conditions. Thus, even if the galaxy has many colonies, Earth may be in an uncolonized region.

The Fermi paradox assumes a highly unlikely similarity among all alien civilizations. It assumes motives of all aliens are the same and that alien and human motives are similar. It assumes these civilizations do not change over millions or billions of years. Even looking at our single sample—humanity—it is obvious this is not the case. Human civilizations change and even die. And, of course, many planets may have bacterial or other simple life, but not civilizations.

THE DRAKE EQUATION

In 1961, astronomer Frank Drake developed an equation to estimate the number of civilizations in the Milky Way galaxy advanced enough to emit signals humans could detect. Drake's equation listed the factors necessary for these civilizations to develop and multiplied them together to give N, the probable number of such civilizations. The Drake equation, and the meaning of each factor, is:

$$N = R^* \times f_p \times n_e \times f_l \times f_i \times f_c \times L$$

$R*$ = number of stars per year formed in the galaxy

f_p = fraction of those stars having solar systems

n_e = number of planets per solar system capable of supporting life

f_l = fraction of those planets actually having life

f_i = fraction of life-bearing planets where intelligent life evolves

f_c = fraction of intelligent civilizations whose technology we can detect

L = average length of time these civilizations have been emitting detectable signals

Many people have estimated N based on assumptions. Drake himself predicted an N of approximately ten thousand. In 1980, famed astronomer Carl Sagan thought it could range from ten to one million or even more, depending on the value of L (the percentage of a planet's lifetime during which it has a communicating civilization). L would be very small if (like humanity) the civilization were warlike, had nuclear weapons, or might otherwise destroy itself quickly. If the civilization learned to live

Astronomer Frank Drake (*center*) is shown in 1962 at the National Radio Astronomy Observatory. Drake is a pioneer in radio astronomy and in the search for extraterrestrial intelligence (SETI).

with its technology and survived for millennia, L would be much larger. A 2008 estimate suggested an N of about twelve thousand—very similar to Drake's original estimate.

But, as Jill Tarter, astronomer at the Search for Extraterrestrial Intelligence (SETI) Research Center at the University of California, Berkeley, points out, there is no "right answer" for the Drake equation because astronomers had to estimate, and often guess at, all of its factors. Only recently, with the discovery of exoplanets, have they begun to provide actual values for some factors. There are now reasonable estimates for R^*, f_p, and n_e. Everything else is a guess. Tarter emphasizes the importance of looking for life elsewhere in our solar system—on Mars, Europa, or Titan. "The discovery of any kind of life there will mean that life will be abundant in the Milky Way, because if life originated twice within this one solar system, it means it was easy," Tarter says, "and given similar conditions elsewhere, life will happen." Even more important is the value for L, the longevity of a civilization. If L is large, N will be large. The SETI project could tell us the relative size of L. If SETI searches only a tiny part of the galaxy and finds life, L must be large—otherwise, life would not have been so easy to find.

In May 2014, SETI representatives spoke before the United States Congress. They described the success of the Kepler spacecraft in finding exoplanets and explained that Kepler data suggest the Milky Way contains approximately one trillion planets (an average of three or more per star). Billions of these are Earth-sized and in the

This is one of twenty-seven dishes of the Very Large Array (VLA) Radio Observatory near Socorro, New Mexico. VLAs are key players in the search for extraterrestrial intelligence (SETI).

habitable zone. According to SETI director Dan Wertheimer, this new information greatly increases the chances of finding intelligent life. That is, the value N, calculated by the Drake equation, rises dramatically.

REVISING THE DRAKE EQUATION

In 2013, Sara Seager, an exoplanet expert from the Massachusetts Institute of Technology, revised the Drake equation. Her revision

PROOF OF ALIEN LIFE?

Professor Milton Wainwright and colleagues from the Universities of Sheffield and Buckingham in the United Kingdom discovered what they called "dragon particles" in 2013. These particles are made of carbon and oxygen—the substance of life—yet they came from dust samples obtained 16.8 miles (27 km) high, in Earth's stratosphere. Wainwright claims they prove life exists in space and is colonizing Earth. He cites as evidence their biological composition; their lack of contamination by

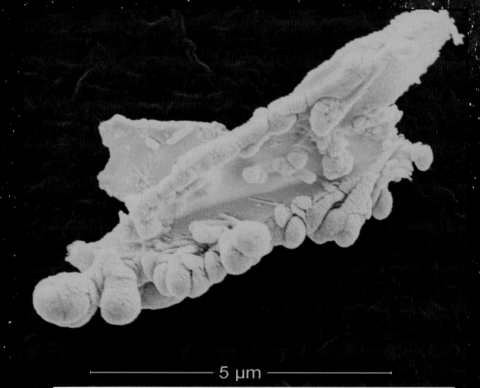

5 μm

Professor Milton Wainwright's team took this photograph of the "dragon particle," which they think is an extraterrestrial life-form. It is ten microns (ten millionths of a meter) in size.

earthly pollen, grass, or pollution particles; and the fact that particles this large have no way to reach that height from Earth (for example, no large volcanic eruptions occurred in the three years prior to the sampling). The majority of scientists are unconvinced. NASA astrobiologist Chris McKay says that concluding these particles are alien life "is a big jump and would require quite extraordinary proof" (for instance, evidence that the particles' biochemistry differs from Earth biochemistry).

focuses not on the presence of technological civilizations, but on the number of planets that might have *any* kind of life. Seager explains that Drake's equation is still valid for locating planets with intelligent life. Her version deals specifically with exoplanet exploration conducted using new technologies to find planets with biosignature gases.

Seager's revision looks like this:

$$N = N^* \times F_Q \times F_{HZ} \times F_O \times F_L \times F_S$$

N = number of planets with detectable signs of life

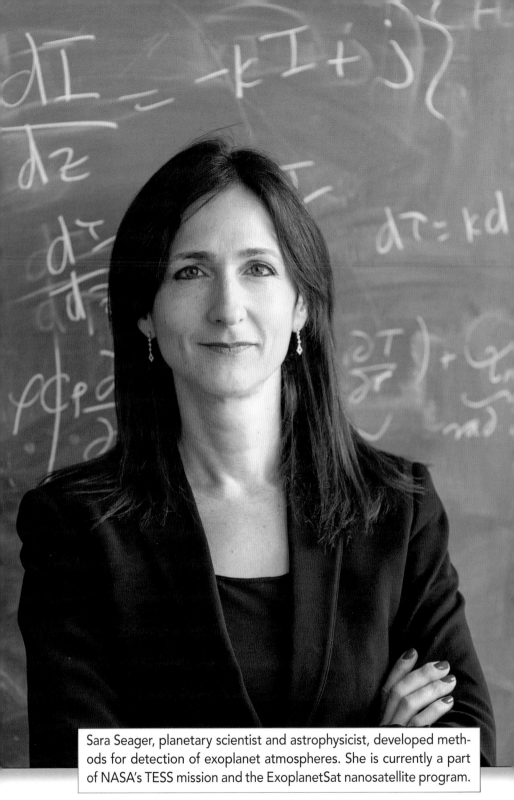

Sara Seager, planetary scientist and astrophysicist, developed methods for detection of exoplanet atmospheres. She is currently a part of NASA's TESS mission and the ExoplanetSat nanosatellite program.

$N*$ = number of stars observed

F_Q = fraction of quiet stars (those with no obvious solar flares)

F_{HZ} = fraction of stars with rocky planets in the habitable zone

F_O = fraction of those planets that we can observe

F_L = fraction of those that have life

F_S = fraction on which life produces a detectable signature gas

Seager concentrated on red dwarfs, which include 75 percent of all stars. Although planets in their habitable zones are tidally locked, with permanent hot and cold sides, those with atmospheres can still circulate heat around the planet, making life possible. Seager felt she had reasonable estimates for all except the last two factors in her equation. In 2013, she calculated that scientists are likely to find two planets with life within a decade.

Researchers looking for alien life are aiming their efforts in three different directions. Some (such as SETI) are looking for advanced, communicating civilizations. Some are seeking simple microbial life within our solar system. Still others will use new technologies to detect microbial life on exoplanets. If Seager is correct, then humans will find life by 2023. Other scientists agree that the hunt is almost over. In July 2014, NASA scientists announced that they expected to find alien life very soon, perhaps on Jupiter's moon Europa. At that time, NASA astronomer Kevin Hand said that within twenty years "we will find out we are not alone in the universe."

CHAPTER FOUR

WHAT WOULD ALIEN LIFE LOOK LIKE?

Chemistry and physics are the same throughout the universe. Scientists use the law of gravity and the speed of light to study stars and exoplanets. They find familiar elements and compounds in exoplanets and their atmospheres. But does biology, the science of life, also follow the same laws everywhere? Do Earth's organic compounds occur on exoplanets? Does alien life have DNA as its genetic material? Does alien life look like Earth life? No one knows for certain. Life processes are based on chemistry, and indications are that life, if it exists "out there," carries out the same life processes as Earth organisms do. But proportions of chemicals vary from planet to planet, and life would likely vary with these proportions.

LIFE ON YOUNG PLANETS

Organic, or carbon-based, life on Earth progressed from simple to complex. Simple microbial cells led to true cells and eventually an explosion of multicellular life that filled all habitats on the planet. This evolutionary progression occurred

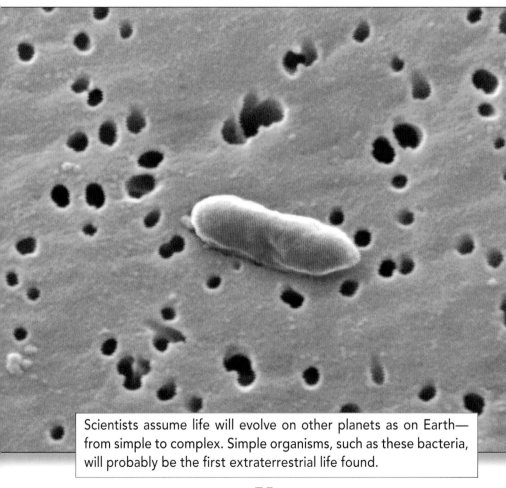

Scientists assume life will evolve on other planets as on Earth—from simple to complex. Simple organisms, such as these bacteria, will probably be the first extraterrestrial life found.

very slowly. Earth formed 4.6 billion years ago (BYA), and the first bacterial cells did not appear until 3.5 BYA. It took another 1.4 billion years for true cells to appear in the fossil record and another 1.6 billion years for multicellular life to become abundant. The first modern humans appeared only 130,000 years ago. The first radio signals were not beamed into space until 1974—less than fifty years ago.

Assuming similar biochemistry, exoplanets would likely follow a similar progression. Single-celled life would be much more common in the universe than multicellular life, and intelligent, communicating life would be rarest of all. Our first glimpse of alien life will probably not be an intelligent civilization, but a biosignature in the atmosphere of an alien world. Life must have energy. It converts a basic energy source—from sunlight, or hydro/geothermal vents, or radioactively decaying elements—into usable energy molecules. Over several billion years, Earth organisms used photosynthesis to convert sunlight into an energy source. They released oxygen, which became 21 percent of the atmosphere—a biosignature of Earth. Other processes might produce planets having biosignatures of water vapor, carbon dioxide, or methane.

SIGNS ALREADY FOUND

The abundance of water, which is necessary for life, makes exobiologists confident of finding alien life. According to NASA's James Green, "water seems to be everywhere." To date, scientists have discovered water on the moon, Mars, and Mercury. Jupiter's moon Europa has a thick coat of ice covering a 60-mile-deep (97 km) ocean, which contains three times more salt water than all of Earth's oceans. The moons Enceladus and Ganymede may also have water, and space telescopes have recently discovered water in the atmospheres of exoplanets.

In addition, the Spitzer Space Telescope has discovered large concentrations of ring-shaped organic compounds—building blocks for organic compounds including DNA, RNA, chlorophyll, and hemoglobin. Mercury, Ganymede, and Enceladus have simpler organic compounds. Meteorites striking Earth contain water (as ice), nitrogen, sulfur, sugars (carbohydrates), amino acids (building blocks of proteins), and some components of the genetic materials DNA and RNA. According to Mars geologist David Blake, "There's no reason that life wouldn't have happened on other solar systems. The ingredients are everywhere we look."

Gullies in the southern highlands of Mars are characteristic of geological forms carved by water. This image was taken by a high-resolution camera on the Mars Reconnaissance Orbiter.

Water worlds in stars' habitable zones are likely places to find alien life. But some planets, far outside typical habitable zones, are also possibilities. These include extremely cold worlds, such as the moons of Jupiter and Saturn. Cold planets might support life by using compounds such as salt, ammonia, or methanol as antifreeze. Life might exist in hydrocarbon lakes or on exoplanets having proportions of carbon, oxygen, and silicon different from Earth proportions. Wherever life turns up, says biogeochemist Ariel Anbar of Arizona State University, "We know we're going to be surprised."

WHAT WOULD LIFE LOOK LIKE?

To the extent that alien habitats resemble Earth habitats, alien organisms may be just as recognizable. But diversity of life-forms is inevitable, given the variation in planets. Given enough time, if one size, shape, behavior, or chemical reaction does not survive, another will likely rise to take its place.

Planets orbiting small red dwarf stars are now considered likely locations for life. Sunlight reaching those planets would be red, rather than yellow, and they would be dimmer than yellow stars. Plants might be much darker, even

SUPER ROACHES

In a 2007 experiment on the Russian Foton-M biosatellite, baby cockroaches that were hatched in space grew and developed faster and were hardier than Earth cockroaches. They also ran faster and were "more energetic and resilient," according to a scientist associated with the project, Dmitry Atyakshin. Roaches can lay eggs several times after one impregnation, and offspring from the second and third batches of eggs, which hatched on Earth, did not show these "super-powers." Scientists are

Russian engineers assemble the Foton-M satellite in the Baikonur Cosmodrome in September 2007. A Soyuz-V rocket carried this satellite, with its "super-roach" experiment, into space.

not sure if the space roaches' abilities resulted from weightlessness, radiation, or another unidentified factor. However, because insects such as cockroaches can survive extreme conditions, many scientists think something similar might evolve on alien planets.

black, because they would need to absorb as much light as possible. Habitable planets are much closer to red suns, so gravity and tidal forces would be much stronger than on Earth, as would solar flares and ultraviolet light reaching the planet. These factors would cause severe stresses that would make life difficult or even prevent it from forming.

Water worlds, such as two recently discovered exoplanets, are likely candidates for life. The planets are 1,200 light years from Earth and are in the habitable zones of their planets. They are 1.4 and 1.6 times the mass of Earth, respectively. Along with water organisms, such planets might evolve winged animals, similar to Earth's birds or flying fish. Flying creatures on a planet with higher gravity or a thicker atmosphere could be larger and more powerful than those on Earth. However, lack of land would make development of technological civilizations unlikely on water planets. Gravity would also have a major effect on life-forms. On a land-based planet, higher gravity might favor four-legged animals over bipedal human types. On a small planet, gravity

THE COLORS OF LIFE

Suns come in different colors. Plants absorb the wavelengths of light available, using some for photosynthesis and reflecting the rest. Photosynthetic pigments would evolve to use the light available. On Earth, plants mostly absorb blue and red light and reflect green, so leaves appear green. Stars hotter than our sun (brighter yellow or blue stars) might have green plants. If a star were much hotter than our sun, its plants would be yellow or red. Red dwarfs have dim light, and plants growing with light from a red dwarf would absorb as many wavelengths as possible. These plants would be very dark, probably black or purple.

would be less stressful, so organisms would be lighter, and many would probably fly.

LIFE WITHOUT WATER?

Water is a solvent and is necessary for chemical reactions, which are necessary for life. Water is also an easy biosignature to identify on alien planets. It would result in life we can recognize because it is similar to Earth life. But some scientists think life can arise using whatever compounds are available. New research suggests carbon dioxide (CO_2) could fulfill water's role. At very high temperatures and pressures, CO_2 can both dissolve substances and help chemical reactions. These conditions occur on Venus and on several recently discovered rocky exoplanets.

Saturn's moon Titan has a temperature of only -290°F (-179°C), so water is frozen solid, but methane is liquid. Titan has a methane cycle rather than a water cycle, and complex reactions involving methane occur in its upper atmosphere. Thus,

In this artist's conception, exoplanet GJ1214b, a Super-Earth, orbits a red dwarf star forty light-years from Earth. GJ1214b has 2.7 times the radius of Earth and 6.5 times its mass.

life might be possible on methane-based planets, which would be much colder than Earth. Like Titan, these worlds might orbit far from yellow stars such as our sun. Methane worlds would orbit much closer to red dwarf stars. Astronomers do not know what life might be like on methane-based planets or how to search for it. Studies of Titan may provide the key.

Titan, the largest of Saturn's sixty-two moons, peeks from behind two of Saturn's rings. Titan's hazy atmosphere consists of natural gas (methane); it also has high, wispy clouds of ice.

WEIRD LIFE

Many scientists assume alien life will be carbon-based, like Earth life, and may even look like Earth life. But is this necessarily true? Biologists have considered the possibility of silicon-based life. Like carbon, silicon can form long chains by binding to itself and to oxygen, allowing formation of very large molecules. The waste product of carbon respiration is the gas carbon dioxide. But silicon-based organisms would produce solid silicon dioxide, or silica, the main constituent of sandstone, sand, and quartz. Science fiction abounds with references to silicon-based life. One is the rocklike Horta, from the *Star Trek* series. Another, in Stanley Weisbaum's novel *A Martian Odyssey*, lives half a million years and breathes by releasing a brick every ten minutes. Astrobiologist Dirk Schulze-Makuch points out that silicon-based life is unlikely on Earth-type planets, where carbon and oxygen are abundant and most silica is trapped in rocks. However, it might occur in situations where these elements are less abundant and temperatures are high enough to produce molten silicate rocks.

Dr. Kenneth Nealson of the University of Southern California and his research group have even found "alien" life-forms on Earth—specifically, electric bacteria. In typical Earth metabolism, an organism receives electrons during breakdown of food. It passes those electrons to a receptor (usually oxygen) to complete an electric circuit and provide energy. At the bottom of New York's Oneida Lake, Nealson discovered electric bacteria that obtain energy from carbohydrates (as typical organisms do) but release electrons by "breathing rocks." Tiny chemical wires in the organisms' outer membranes directly touch rocks containing manganese oxide, which completes the electric circuit. Researcher Annette Rowe has since isolated more than one thousand strains of electric bacteria from Catalina Harbor in California. Some of them not only breathe but also eat electricity. They live on electrodes alone—no carbon necessary. Electric life is another type of extremophile that

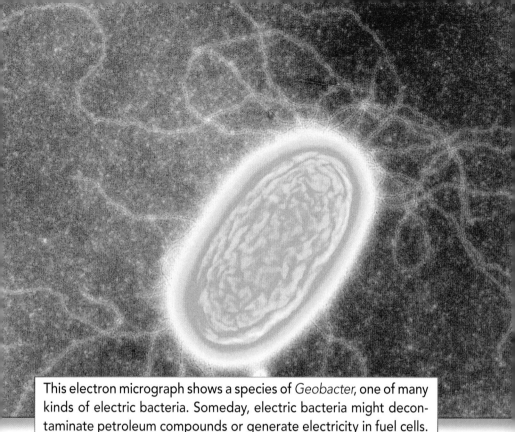

This electron micrograph shows a species of *Geobacter,* one of many kinds of electric bacteria. Someday, electric bacteria might decontaminate petroleum compounds or generate electricity in fuel cells.

exobiologists can add to their list of potential alien life-forms.

Alien life might look like Earth life or be very different. At this point, exobiologists can only speculate and continue to explore. But sometime soon, at least one planet or moon may give up its secrets, and humans will discover at least one life-form that is truly alien.

CHAPTER FIVE

HOW LIKELY IS INTELLIGENT LIFE?

NASA expects to find some kind of alien life within the next decade or two. Seth Shostak of SETI thinks that by 2040 we will likely have discovered *intelligent* alien life. By that time, the Kepler Space Telescope will have scanned about a million galaxies, rather than the few thousand scanned during its first five years. Shostak thinks that, within the tens of billions of worlds where life might appear, some will be producing electromagnetic signals we can recognize. If that happens, what can we expect?

IDENTIFYING ALIEN INTELLIGENCE

Humans have been looking for electromagnetic signals from space for only a few decades—an instant compared to the age of the universe. These signals captured by radiotelescopes are the only way SETI can currently search for alien intelligence. But does all intelligent life in the universe communicate this way? And can we understand their signals?

Lord Martin Rees, astronomer and president of Britain's Royal Society, says, "I suspect there could be life and intelligence out there in forms we can't conceive. Just as a chimpanzee can't understand quantum theory, it could be there are aspects of reality that are beyond the capacity of our brains." Biologist Denise Herzing of Florida Atlantic University is using her thirty-year study of dolphin intelligence and social structure to help scientists rethink alien intelligence. Her 2014 project, called COMPLEX (Complexity of Markers for Profiling Life in Exobiology), compares five types of intelligences (dolphin, octopus, bee, microbe, and machine) against each other, rather than against humans. Herzing worked with astrobiologists and a computer scientist to develop her method.

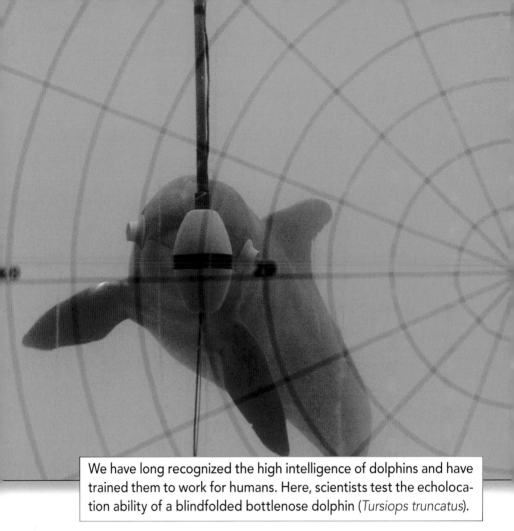

We have long recognized the high intelligence of dolphins and have trained them to work for humans. Here, scientists test the echolocation ability of a blindfolded bottlenose dolphin (*Tursiops truncatus*).

Previous studies compared nonhuman to human intelligence. They looked for physical features such as large brains and behavioral traits such as problem solving and language. COMPLEX bases its studies on encephalization quotient or EQ (ratio of brain mass to body mass), communication signals, individual complexity, social complexity, and interspecies interaction. These are all aspects of information processing but not necessarily of human intelligence. Computer analysis showed that different animals scored high on different aspects. Herzing sees COMPLEX as a way to compare types of intelligence without depending on exclusively human characteristics. In future exercises, she will compare more types of intelligences and more characteristics—essentially making COMPLEX more complex. Scientists hope this study will help decrease human bias when trying to recognize alien intelligence.

HOW LIKELY ARE HUMANOIDS?

Many science fiction aliens look more or less human. Besides intelligence, they share two basic traits with humans: bilateral symmetry (two opposite sides that look the same) and bipedal locomotion (walking upright on two legs). But can we assume aliens would look like humans? Some people say they would, based on the theory of panspermia, which says life on

Earth was "seeded" from space by the arrival of microbes or organic molecules. This would mean the DNA in all organisms originated outside Earth. Seeding could happen by the settling of interstellar dust or by extremophile microbes traveling on asteroids, meteorites, or comets. Some think panspermia could transfer life among planets both within and between solar systems. Several Earth meteorites have contained what look like fossilized microbes. But most people are not convinced. These structures are smaller than Earth bacteria, and many doubt that even extremophiles could survive outer space. However, if panspermia did occur, it would probably only transfer microbes.

Evolution of humanoids on other planets is more likely to occur by the process of convergent evolution, in which similar forms develop independently in different locations. This process would require billions of years, plus environmental stresses similar to those on Earth. Certain characteristics (opposable thumbs, upright posture, a head covered with sense organs, and warm-bloodedness) gave humans

Here, an artist shows a comet crashing into Earth. Comet, meteorite, or asteroid impacts might deliver extremophiles to Earth, but this would more likely happen by close encounters, not impacts.

a strong survival advantage during evolution. According to James Kasting, professor of geoscience at Penn State University, these characteristics would be valuable to organisms on any planet, making them likely to evolve independently. Astrobiologist Steven J. Dick notes that convergent evolution has happened frequently on Earth (for example, similar eyes in vertebrates and octopuses, and wings in insects, birds, and bats). Evolutionary biologist Richard Dawkins further points out that, although evolution is random, species do tend to evolve toward "fitness peaks"; that is, over many generations, they get better at specialized tasks (for example, building a spider web). These factors suggest that humanoid characteristics might also develop on other planets.

WHAT ABOUT NONHUMANOIDS?

Not everyone thinks aliens would look human. Evolutionary biologist Stephen Jay Gould thought alien life would look totally different from Earth life. Because evolution is random, he said, even if we "re-ran the tape" on Earth, and evolution began again, humans would not form a second time. Given the staggering odds of any specific life-form evolving even on Earth, many people find it highly unlikely that Earth-like humanoids would arise anywhere else.

Many multicellular body forms arose on Earth, went extinct, and now exist only as fossils. Present-day complex life shows incredible diversity, all based on random rolls of the genetic dice. Most of those diverse species—all plants, animals, and fungi—exist only because of sexual reproduction. How likely is sexual reproduction to develop elsewhere? Great diversity of life seems likely on any planet, but the direction that diversity takes and the way it develops is anyone's guess. At least one astronomer, NASA's Ethan Siegel, thinks the existence of other technological civilizations is even more unlikely. But, he adds, "unlikely events happen, and we know it happened *once*, here. If it happened even one other time, don't you want to know?"

STAR WARS ALIENS

The *Star Wars* movies contain more than 150 alien species, each carefully designed for conditions on different home planets and each having its own physical, mental, and cultural characteristics. The book *The Essential Guide to Alien Species* describes all the species and planets created in the fictional *Star Wars* universe. Many species are bipedal and reminiscent of Earth animals, from big, hairy Wookiees to small, furry Ewoks. Others, such as the huge, sluglike Jabba the Hutt, are based on much less appealing Earth animals. The Jedi master Yoda never named his species and seemed to be one of a kind. If humans begin to encounter alien species, how will these imaginary aliens compare to the real thing?

The Jedi Master Yoda is a master of the Force. His wisdom, skill, and high intelligence make him one of the most renowned—and most quoted—of Star Wars characters.

CAN WE COMMUNICATE?

Our ability to communicate with intelligent aliens would depend in large part on *how* intelligent they were and what type of intelligence they have. It is safe to assume the intelligence of any aliens we encounter would either be similar to, or much greater than, human intelligence. Communicating with aliens having primate characteristics similar to our own would likely be much easier than communicating with higher, or more alien, types of intelligence. Some scientists think intelligent alien species might have social and behavioral characteristics in common with humans, as well as physical ones. Ecologist and geographer Jared Diamond has listed various human characteristics we share with other primates. These include highly social behavior combined with a tendency to form hierarchies, risk-taking behavior, intense curiosity, and superior language and conceptual skills. George Dvorsky, Canadian futurist and bioethicist, thinks that, even if intelligent aliens are not primates, they may also have some or all of these characteristics. This would give them much in common with humans, making understanding and communication possible.

But some experts, including NASA historian Steven J. Dick, think the dominant life-form in the universe might be "post-biological," or machine intelligence. Because Dick thinks the human brain has a limited ability to absorb and store knowledge, he has proposed the Intelligence Principle, which states:

THE MAINTENANCE, IMPROVEMENT AND PERPETU-ATION OF KNOWLEDGE AND INTELLIGENCE IS THE CENTRAL DRIVING FORCE OF CULTURAL EVOLU-TION, AND TO THE EXTENT INTELLIGENCE CAN BE IMPROVED, IT WILL BE IMPROVED.

According to both Dick and Dvorsky, this "improvement"—that is, the trend toward machine intelligence—is currently just beginning in human society, through developments in fields such as genetics, cybernetics, molecular nano-technology, cognitive science, and information technology. If a majority of alien intelligences are indeed cyborgs, our ability to communicate with them—at least at present—may be very limited.

Still, some scientists are taking a practical view, trying to determine how we would communicate with aliens. In 2014, a NASA e-book explored how anthropologists and archaeologists unravel different Earth cultures. They considered how the same techniques might apply to alien cultures and languages. For example, like earthlings, aliens could possibly have many different cultures on a single planet. They would likely have different sense organs, so they would experience environments differently, resulting in various types of communication. For example, alien communication might rely more strongly on sight than on sound, as ours does. Artificial intelligence expert Dr. John Elliott considers alien communication from a more mathematical viewpoint. He decodes human languages by breaking down their structures. Sounds or words, Elliott says, make each language different, but the underlying structures and patterns of languages are all very similar. He thinks his decoding methods might be used to break down alien languages and help us communicate. These approaches assume aliens will be biological, not machine-based, but Elliot's mathematical approach might also help decode machine intelligences.

SHOULD WE CONTACT ALIENS?

Now that research has shown the huge number of exoplanets out there, scientists are hotly debating whether humans should actively search for intelligent alien life—that is, should we send our own messages and look for responses—as well as passively search for incoming broadcasts? SETI astronomer Seth Shostak likens this process, called active SETI, to "tossing a bottle into the cosmic ocean."

Some think actively seeking out alien life might threaten Earth. We have no way to predict alien motives or behavior. Aliens intelligent enough to intercept our messages and decode them would likely have better technology than humans do. If these aliens were hostile or aggressive, humanity would be unprotected. In 1998, cosmologist Stephen Hawking commented that when an advanced civilization meets a less advanced one, things seldom turn out well for the less advanced culture. In 2015, astrophysicist and science fiction author David Brin agreed. Brin fears that, instead of E.T., we might attract the aliens from *Independence Day*. He thinks scientists should stop trying to contact aliens until they can give valid reasons why contact would not endanger humans.

Others want to start active SETI now. They think this may be the only way to show that we are not alone, and we may benefit from contact with aliens. The late Carl Sagan agreed with this approach. Sagan felt alien civilizations that had survived long enough to travel the galaxy would not be overly aggressive or they would already have killed each other. Because they would be more advanced than humans are, they would not fear us and therefore would not be aggressive. Scientists committed to active SETI are now discussing what messages to send. Early satellites carried very short messages. Voyager 1, launched in 1977, carried a tiny "golden record" containing

Voyager 2, shown here, launched from Cape Canaveral in 1977. Project manager John Casani shows an American flag and the "golden record," which Voyager carried out of the solar system.

sounds and images of Earth life. It finally left our solar system for interstellar space in 2012. Shostak recommends sending "big data" into space—for example, the entire contents of the Internet. A powerful laser traveling at light speed could send this much information in only a few days. Just as Sagan did, Shostak dismisses the fears of those who expect hostile aliens. He says, "The universe beckons, and we can do better than to declare that future generations should endlessly tremble at the sight of the stars."

CHAPTER SIX

WHAT'S NEXT IN THE SEARCH FOR ALIEN LIFE?

What happens next in the search for extraterrestrial life? What are the long-term strategies? The future search for alien life will occur on two fronts: within the solar system and in the larger universe. Within the solar system, future NASA missions will target solar system bodies most likely to have life. This includes Mars and several moons of Jupiter and Saturn.

SEEKING LIFE ON MARS

Earlier Mars missions located signs of water. NASA's current Mars exploration strategy, "Seek Signs of Life," began with the Curiosity rover, which landed in 2012. Curiosity is seeking signs of organic molecules by collecting and chemically analyzing rock and soil samples. MAVEN, or Mars Atmospheric and Volatile Evolution, was launched in 2013. It orbits Mars, collecting information on the Martian atmosphere and climate. This data will help determine if life has ever arisen on Mars.

NASA's InSight mission, scheduled to land in September 2016, will study how the planet formed. It will dig deep into the Mars interior to measure seismology and heat flow. NASA will also participate in the ExoMars Program (Exobiology on Mars), a joint European Space Agency

The "Seek Signs of Life" strategy is one of many long-term strategies. It focuses on Mars's ability to support life by studying its environment. Each mission will ask different scientific questions.

and Roscosmos (Russian) venture. The 2016 ExoMars Trace Gas Orbiter (TGO) mission will measure methane and other atmospheric gases present in very low quantities. These gases are possible biosignatures. The 2018 mission is a rover, the MOMA (Mars Organic Molecule Analyzer). NASA will provide a mass spectrometer and electronic components for MOMA, which will study organic molecules to try to determine if life exists (or has existed) on Mars.

Finally, as part of the Mars Exploration Program, NASA plans to launch a new robotic science rover in 2020. This rover's seven science instruments will study habitability on Mars and help prepare astronauts for in-person Mars visits.

SEEKING LIFE ON MOONS

According to NASA's Kevin Hand, Jupiter's moon Europa has the "three keystones for habitability"—water, access to elements required to build life, and energy sources (including tidal forces between Jupiter and Europa, geothermal energy, and oxidants such as hydrogen peroxide). In 2022, NASA plans

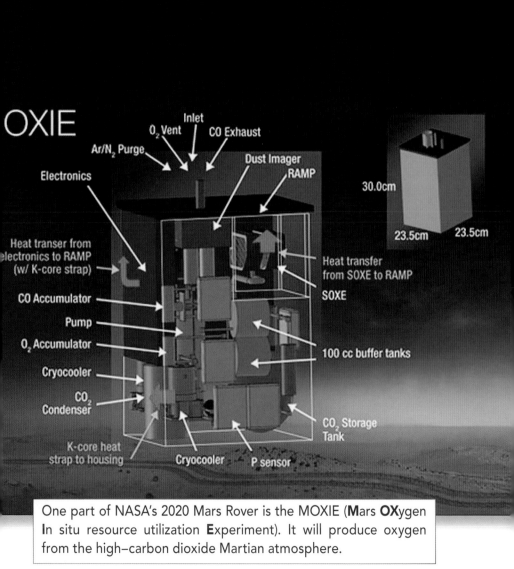

One part of NASA's 2020 Mars Rover is the MOXIE (**M**ars **OX**ygen **I**n situ resource utilization **E**xperiment). It will produce oxygen from the high–carbon dioxide Martian atmosphere.

to launch a flyby mission to Europa. The probe Europa Clipper would orbit Jupiter and make forty-five flybys at altitudes varying from 16 miles to 1,700 miles (25–2,735 km). It would measure and map Europa's icy surface and study its subsurface ocean to determine depth, salinity, and other characteristics. Scientists hope the Europa Clipper might also sample the water plumes shooting from Europa's southern pole, analyzing them for amino acids and other biosignatures. Europe is also planning a 2022 mission to Europa, the Jupiter Icy Moon Mission. This mission would also study the moons Ganymede and Callisto.

In the long term, scientists hope to study Saturn's moons Titan and Enceladus. Titan appears to be much like a cold, primitive Earth. In early 2015, NASA scientists unveiled a concept for a submersible that would explore Titan's methane seas. It would make periodic trips to the surface to send data back to Earth. The German Aerospace Center launched a mission, the Enceladus Explorer, to Enceladus in 2012. They hope eventually to land on

NASA hopes to launch its mission to Europa, called the Europa Multiple-Flyby Mission, in the 2020s. This is an artist's conception of the flyby orbiter, originally called the Europa Clipper.

Enceladus and use an ice probe to melt through the ice to the watery core, which the probe would sample and test.

TELESCOPES AND THE LARGER UNIVERSE

New telescopes will continue the search for life outside the solar system. The Kepler Space Telescope, launched in 2009, has found many exoplanets, but it views only a small sliver of the sky. A new space-based telescope, the 2017 Transiting Exoplanet Survey Satellite (TESS), will cover four hundred times as much sky as Kepler. It will search bright stars close to Earth, specifically looking for small, rocky planets in the habitable zone. TESS's instruments will study new planets' orbits, masses, densities, and atmospheric compositions. The 2018 James Webb Space Telescope will observe past and present formation of galaxies, stars, and planetary systems and will be the next generation's "workhorse" telescope, eventually taking over for the Hubble Telescope.

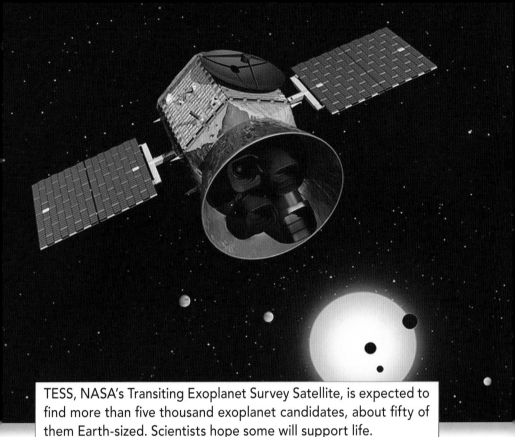

TESS, NASA's Transiting Exoplanet Survey Satellite, is expected to find more than five thousand exoplanet candidates, about fifty of them Earth-sized. Scientists hope some will support life.

Scientists from University College London (UCL) and Surrey Satellite Technology are planning a space mission called Twinkle, scheduled for launch by 2020. The Twinkle satellite will orbit 450 miles (724 km) above Earth. Its single telescope will have two spectrometers measuring a broad range of light wavelengths. Twinkle scientists will study exoplanets for biosignatures including oxygen, hydrogen, methane, ammonia, carbon dioxide, sulfur compounds, and water vapor.

Ground-based telescopes last longer and are cheaper and easier to maintain than space telescopes. Three new ground-based telescopes should be operating by about 2025: the Giant Magellan Telescope (GMT) and the European Extremely Large Telescope, both located in Chile, as well as the Thirty Meter Telescope in Hawaii. These telescopes will have mirror diameters of 80.4, 128.9, and 98.4 feet (24.5, 39.3, and 30 meters), respectively. The largest mirror currently in operation is 34 feet (10.4 m). These huge new telescopes will track spectral changes to identify changing seasons and biosignatures of exoplanets.

LOOKING FARTHER AHEAD

Another space-based telescope will launch in 2030. The Advanced Technology Large-Aperture Space Telescope (ATLAST) will have primary mirrors ranging from 26.5 to 52.5 feet (8–16 m) in diameter. The smallest will be larger than most telescopes and two thousand times more sensitive than the Hubble Telescope, astronomy's current space workhorse. ATLAST will be a "life finder." It will analyze the light spectra of exoplanets for biosignatures including water, ozone, and methane.

Astronomers are also working on new ways to study exoplanets. ExoplanetSat is a tiny "nano-satellite" containing a telescope about the size of a loaf of bread. Each nanosatellite would monitor a single bright star continuously for two years, making it easier to find exoplanets. Another concept is the "star shade." Currently, astronomers must observe exoplanets indirectly because the glare from a planet's star hides the planet. The star shade is a flower-shaped screen. It is engineered to fly away from the telescope and be precisely oriented to block out the star's light. This removes the glare so the telescope can view the planet directly.

HOW WOULD HUMAN LIFE CHANGE?

First, we must find life on other worlds. But astronomer and historian Steven Dick wants to understand how finding alien life would affect the human worldview. He points out that society and even scientists are slow to accept any discovery. For example, although a Martian meteorite discovered in Antarctica in 1996 appears to contain biological structures, scientists still cannot agree if it is alive. If we discover and accept life on another planet, this would profoundly affect biology, Dick says. Suddenly, biology would be a universal science, no longer limited to Earth.

Dick also considers psychological, social, and ethical implications of contact with intelligent aliens. One aspect of interest is the issue of "astro-ethics," or how humans would treat alien life. Would aliens have equal or lesser status than humans? How would we judge (and respond to) alien intelligence? Dick observes that, in contact between Earth cultures, some results were devastating (European explorer Cortés meeting the Aztecs) and others more fruitful (Canadian fur traders and Native Americans in the 1800s). Communicating ideas is especially difficult without a common language, and some

ARE ALIENS ALREADY HERE?

People see thousands of unidentified flying objects, or UFOs, every year. Most are explainable, but about 5 percent defy classification. People who report them are dismissed or ridiculed. In 2010, a group of thirteen retired generals, scientists, and space experts released the COMETA Report, published in France. COMETA analyzed UFO encounters by military and civilian pilots (and in some cases, hundreds of civilians) around the world. Pilots and other professionals have observed these objects at close range, photographed them, and tracked them on radar. Their maneuvers seem to defy physics: they accelerate to tremendous speeds, make sharp and instant right-angle turns, and hover soundlessly in midair. The report concluded the objects were "completely unknown flying machines with exceptional performances that are guided by a natural or artificial intelligence." That is, they are unknowns, not jokes.

concepts do not translate well. But humans have successfully transmitted information across cultures. Some scientists assume we could use mathematics as a universal language to communicate with aliens, but others fear even mathematics will differ. To consider such issues, Dick hosted a symposium in 2014, cosponsored by NASA and the Library of Congress, titled "Preparing for Discovery." He says, "It's a good idea to do this, to foresee what might happen before it occurs."

Humans will likely discover some type of extraterrestrial life within the next decade or two. SETI scientists may even contact intelligent alien life—or they may contact us. If the intelligent life is much more advanced than humans are (a very likely situation), how will we respond? Will we achieve a breakthrough in our own understanding of ourselves? Will we collaborate and learn from our new galactic neighbors? No matter what happens, the coming decades will hold excitement and adventure for "alien hunters"—and for all humans.

GLOSSARY

ACTIVE SETI Deliberately trying to contact alien civilizations by sending specially prepared messages, as opposed to passively searching space for incoming signals.

AEROBIC Containing oxygen (as an aerobic atmosphere) or requiring oxygen for respiration (as an aerobic bacterium).

ALIEN LIFE (EXTRATERRESTRIAL LIFE) Non-Earth life, or life occurring outside Earth, either in space or on other planets or moons; so far, no verified alien life has been discovered.

ANAEROBIC Lacking oxygen (as an anaerobic atmosphere) or not requiring oxygen for respiration or being poisoned by it (as an anaerobic bacterium).

ATP Adenosine triphosphate; the organic molecule that is the "quick energy" source for all living organisms; it is produced when food is metabolized and used to carry out life activities.

BIOSIGNATURE A chemical element or compound that might indicate life, occurring in the atmospheres of planets or moons; examples include water, oxygen, and chlorophyll.

CONVERGENT EVOLUTION Process by which organisms having similar forms develop independently in separate locations (one explanation for development of humanoids on other planets).

DNA Deoxyribonucleic acid; the organic molecule that carries genetic information for an organism and is passed on to new generations; found in all living organisms on Earth.

DRAKE EQUATION An equation developed by astronomer Frank Drake in 1961, used to estimate N, the number of likely intelligent civilizations in the universe; includes factors necessary for civilizations to develop, but astronomers lack specific values for most factors.

ENCEPHALIZATION QUOTIENT (EQ) The proportion of brain size to body size, or the size of the brain compared to the body; a high EQ is assumed to indicate a high level of intelligence.

EVOLUTION Genetic change in populations

of organisms resulting from adaptation to environmental changes and occurring by the process of natural selection.

EXOBIOLOGIST A scientist who searches for life on planets or moons other than Earth and who studies the effects of extra-terrestrial environments on organisms.

EXOPLANET Extrasolar planet; a planet orbiting a star outside our solar system.

EXTREMOPHILE An organism capable of living under extreme conditions of temperature, pressure, pH, radiation, drought, salinity, or starvation; classified by the extreme conditions for which it is adapted (for example, a thermophile).

EYEBALL PLANET A tidally locked planet (with constant day and night sides) that looks like an eyeball with the pupil side pointing at its star; some eyeball planets might have a temperate region at the boundary between the night and day sides that can support life.

FERMI PARADOX The idea, first expressed by Enrico Fermi in 1950, that if intelligent civilizations exist elsewhere in the universe, they should have found Earth by now.

GOLDILOCKS ZONE (HABITABLE ZONE) A region of space around a star that is not too hot and not too cold, but has just the right temperature for Earth-like life to exist.

METABOLISM The process of chemically breaking down food to release ATP energy for organism activity.

ORGANIC Carbon-based; composed of large molecules formed from carbon and five other major elements; characteristic of all Earth life; in contrast, inorganic molecules are nonliving.

PANSPERMIA The idea that life on Earth has been "seeded" with DNA from space through colonization by microbes or chemical precursors of life.

REPLICATION The process by which an organism copies its own genetic material (DNA) and passes it on to future generations through reproduction.

SETI The search for extraterrestrial intelligence, an exploratory science seeking signatures of technology as evidence of intelligent life in space; research occurs in many places, including Harvard University, the University of California, Berkeley, and the SETI Institute in Mountain View, California.

TIDALLY LOCKED A situation in which the same side of a planet always faces its star, so one side of the planet is always hot and light, while the other side is always cold and dark.

TRANSIT METHOD A method of locating an exoplanet by observing the change in brightness of its star as the planet passes between the star and Earth.

FOR MORE INFORMATION

Canadian Astrobiology Network (CAN)
c/o Neil Banerjee
University of Western Ontario
Biological & Geological Sciences Building,
Room 1026
1151 Richmond Street North
London, ON N6A 5B7
Canada
(519) 661-3187
Website: http://astrobiology.uwo.ca

The Canadian Astrobiology Network is a group of Canadian institutions and researchers in the field of astrobiology. Its goal is to encourage cooperation between Canadian researchers and researchers in the United States and around the world.

Canadian Astrobiology Training Program
(CATP)
c/o Yella Jovich-Zahirovich
McGill University, Macdonald Campus
Faculty of Agricultural and Environmental Sciences
Department of Natural Resource Sciences
MS Building, 3rd Floor, Room R3-039
21,111 Lakeshore Road
Ste-Anne-de-Bellevue, QC H9X 3V9

Canada
(514) 398 7824
Website: http://create-astrobiology.mcgill.ca
The CATP is cross-disciplinary and multi-institutional and is located at McGill University, McMaster University, University of Western Ontario, University of Toronto, and the University of Winnipeg.

Center for Astrobiology
University of Arizona College of Science
Steward Observatory
The University of Arizona
933 North Cherry Avenue
Tucson, AZ 85718
(520) 621-6963
Website: http://astrobiology.arizona.edu
The Center for Astrobiology carries out interdisciplinary research and education in astrobiology. It combines research from astronomy, planetary science, chemistry, geology, and biology.

European Space Agency (ESA)/European
    Space Research Institute (ESRIN)
Via Galileo Galilei
Casella Postale 64
00044 Frascati RM
Italy

Website: http://www.esa.int

The European Space Agency is similar to NASA in the United States. This cooperative group from several European countries conducts space missions and research, and its website includes news and educational materials for teachers, students, and citizens.

National Aeronautics and Space Administration (NASA)
Public Communications Office
NASA Headquarters
300 E Street SW, Suite 5R30
Washington, DC 20546
(202) 358-0001
Website: http://www.nasa.gov

NASA is the United States space agency, responsible for space flight and exploration of the solar system and larger universe by telescope, satellite, and probes to various celestial bodies. Its astrobiology division involves missions to study life on bodies in and out of the solar system.

The Planetary Society
85 South Grand Avenue
Pasadena, CA 91105
(626) 793-5100
Website: http://www.planetary.org

The Planetary Society is a nonprofit organization designed to empower the world's citizens to advance space science and space exploration. It has information on space and space exploration, videos and blogs, and a kids' section featuring Bill Nye, the Science Guy.

SETI Institute
189 Bernardo Avenue, Suite 100
Mountain View, CA 94043
(650) 961-6633
Website: http://www.seti.org

The SETI Institute is a nonprofit scientific and educational organization designed to explore and understand life in the universe. Scientists use satellites and telescopes to search for life in the universe. SETI has many educational resources for students and teachers.

The SETI League, Inc.
433 Liberty Street
Little Ferry, NJ 07643
(201) 641-1770
Website: http://www.setileague.org

The SETI League is a membership-funded international organization dedicated to privatizing the search for extraterrestrial intelligence. It seeks to coordinate the use of thousands of small radiotelescopes to detect microwaves from other intelligent civilizations.

Space Telescope Science Institute (STSI)
Johns Hopkins University
3700 San Martin Drive
Baltimore, MD 21218
(410) 338-4700
Website: http://www.stsci.edu/institute

The STSI, located on the Johns Hopkins University campus, is operated by the Association of Universities for Research in Astronomy (AURA) for NASA.

WEBSITES

Because of the changing nature of Internet links, Rosen Publishing has developed an online list of websites related to the subject of this book. This site is updated regularly. Please use this link to access the list:

http://www.rosenlinks.com/SOE/Life

FOR FURTHER READING

Aguilar, David A. *Alien Worlds: Your Guide to Extraterrestrial Life* (National Geographic Kids). Washington, DC: National Geographic Children's Books, 2013.

Bortz, Fred. *Astrobiology* (Cool Science). Minneapolis, MN: Lerner Publications, 2008.

Brake, Mark, and Colin Jack. *Alien Hunter's Handbook: How to Look for Extra-Terrestrial Life*. London, England: Kingfisher (Houghton-Mifflin), 2012.

Catling, David C. *Astrobiology: A Very Short Introduction* (Very Short Introductions). New York, NY: Oxford University Press, 2014.

Coppens, Philip. *Ancient Aliens: Close Encounters with Human History* (Conspiracies and Cover-ups). New York, NY: Rosen Publishing, 2015.

Dartnell, Lewis. *Astrobiology: Exploring Life in the Universe* (Contemporary Issues). New York, NY: Rosen Publishing, 2011.

Dudzinski, Kathleen M., and Toni Frohoff. *Dolphin Mysteries: Unlocking the Secrets of Communication*. New Haven, CT: Yale University Press, 2008.

Editors of *Time* Magazine. *TIME New Frontiers of Space: From Mars to the Edge of the universe.* New York, NY: Time, 2013.

Grayson, Robert. *Exploring Space* (The Story of Exploration). Minneapolis, MN: Abdo Publishing, 2014.

Halls, Kelly Milner. *Alien Investigation. Searching for the Truth About UFOs and Aliens.* Minneapolis, MN: Millbrook Press, 2012.

Kallen, Stuart A. *The Search for Extraterrestrial Life* (Extraterrestrial Life). San Diego, CA: Referencepoint Press, 2011.

Morrison, Philip, John Billingham, and John Wolfe, eds. *The Search for Extraterrestrial Intelligence.* Mountain View, CA: National Aeronautics and Space Administration, 1977.

Sagan, Carl. *Cosmos.* New York, NY: Ballantine Books (Random House), 2013.

Schulze-Makuch, Dirk, and David Darling. *We Are Not Alone: Why We Have Already Found Extraterrestrial Life.* London, England: Oneworld Publications, 2011.

Shea, Therese. *Investigating UFOs and Aliens* (Understanding the Paranormal). New York,

NY: Rosen Publishing, 2015.

Silverstein, Alvin, Virginia Silverstein, and Laura Silverstein Nunn. *The Universe* (Revised edition). Minneapolis, MN: Twenty-First Century Books, 2009.

Turner, Pamela S. *Life on Earth—and Beyond: An Astrobiologist's Quest*. Watertown, MA: Charlesbridge Publishing, 2008.

Ward, D. J. *Seven Wonders of Space Phenomena* (Seven Wonders). Minneapolis, MN: Twenty-First Century Books, 2011.

Webb, Stephen. *If the Universe Is Teeming with Aliens… Where Is Everybody? Seventy-Five Solutions to the Fermi Paradox and the Problem of Extraterrestrial Life* (Science and Fiction). Second edition. Cham, Switzerland: Springer International Publishing, 2015.

BIBLIOGRAPHY

Daily Galaxy. "Recognizing Extraterrestrial Intelligence—There Could Be Life and Intelligence Out There in Forms We Can't Conceive." January 27, 2014. Retrieved May 16, 2015 (http://www.dailygalaxy .com/my_weblog/2014/01/recognizing-extraterrestrial -intelligence-there-could-be-life-and-intelligence-out -there-in-forms-we.html).

Department of Paleobiology. "Eukaryotes and the First Multicellular Life Forms." Smithsonian National Museum of Natural History. Retrieved May 11, 2015 (http://paleobiology.si.edu/geotime/main/htmlversion /proterozoic3.html).

Dvorsky, George. "What to Expect from Aliens When We Make First Contact." io9, July 2, 2015. Retrieved July 3, 2015 (http://io9.com/what-to-expect-from-aliens-when -we-make-first-contact-1715402190).

Encrenaz, Thérèse. *Planets: Ours and Others. From Earth to Exoplanets.* Hackensack, NJ: World Scientific Publishing, 2014.

Finkel, Elizabeth. "Life on Mars—the Evidence Mounts." *Cosmos Magazine*, January 12, 2015. Retrieved May 5, 2015 (https://cosmosmagazine.com/space/life-mars -%E2%80%93-evidence-mounts).

Gertz, Emily. "How We'll Talk to Aliens." *Popular Science*, May 27, 2014. Retrieved May 20, 2015 (http://www .popsci.com/article/science/how-well-talk-aliens).

Hall, Shannon. "Life After Kepler: Upcoming Exoplanet Missions." November 4, 2013. Retrieved May 22, 2015 (http://www.universetoday.com/105992/life-after -kepler-upcoming-exoplanet-missions).

Harris, William. "What Are the Odds There Is Life in Outer Space?" HowStuffWorks.com, August 11, 2008. Retrieved May 8, 2015 (http://science.howstuffworks.com/space /aliens-ufos/extraterrestrial-life-odds.htm).

Howell, Elizabeth. "How Earth's 'Extremophiles' Could Aid Alien Life Search." Space.com, October 21, 2013. Retrieved Apr. 20, 2015 (http://www.space.com/23234 -earth-extremophiles-alien-life-search.html).

Howell, Elizabeth. "How Would the World Change if We Found Extraterrestrial Life?" Phys.org, January 29, 2015. Retrieved May 24, 2015 (http://phys.org /news/2015-01-world-extraterrestrial-life.html).

Jenkins, Jon A., et al. "Discovery and Validation of Kepler-452b: A 1.6-$R_\oplus$ Super-Earth Exoplanet in the Habitable Zone of a G2 Star." *Astronomical Journal*, July 23, 2015. Retrieved July 23, 2015 (http://www.nasa.gov /sites/default/files/atoms/files/ms-r1b.pdf).

Jet Propulsion Laboratory. "Exoplanet History—From Intuition to Discovery." NASA, California Institute of Technology. Retrieved May 6, 2015 (http://planetquest .jpl.nasa.gov/page/history).

NASA Mars Exploration. "Programs and Missions. Future." 2013. Retrieved May 23, 2015 (http://mars.nasa.gov /programmissions/missions/future).

NASA Mars Exploration. "Programs and Missions. Overview." 2013. Retrieved May 23, 2015 (http://mars.nasa .gov/programmissions/overview).

NASA Science. "The Goldilocks Zone." NASA Science, April 6, 2011. Retrieved May 3, 2011 (http://science .nasa.gov/science-news/science-at-nasa/2003/02oct _goldilocks).

O'Neill, Ian. "Why the Hunt for Extraterrestrial Life Is Important." *Discovery News*, December 5, 2013. Retrieved April 16, 2015 (http://news.discovery.com /space/alien-life-exoplanets/why-the-hunt-for -extraterrestrial-life-is-important-131205.htm).

Overbye, Dennis. "NASA Says Data Reveals an Earth-Like Planet, Kepler 452b." *New York Times*, July 23, 2015.

Retrieved July 23, 2015 (http://www.nytimes
.com/2015/07/24/science/space/kepler-data-reveals
-what-might-be-best-goldilocks-planet-yet.html?_r=0).

Powell, Corey S. "Have We Found Alien Life?" *Popular
Science*, February 2015. New York, NY: Popular Science
Co. 32–39, 70.

Sengupta, Sujan. *Worlds Beyond Our Own. The Search for
Habitable Planets*. Cham, Switzerland: Springer International Publishing, 2015.

SETI Institute. "The Drake Equation." 2015. Retrieved May
8, 2015 (http://www.seti.org/drakeequation).

SETI Institute. "Fermi Paradox." 2015. Retrieved May 7,
2015 (http://www.seti.org/seti-institute/project/details
/fermi-paradox).

Shostak, Seth. "Should We Keep a Low Profile in Space?"
New York Times Sunday Review, March 27, 2015.
Retrieved May 20, 2015 (http://www.nytimes.com/2015
/03/28/opinion/sunday/messaging-the-stars.html?
_r=4).

Siegel, Ethan. "Finding the First Signs of Alien Life, and
Why NASA Thinks It's Coming Soon." *Forbes*, April 10,
2015. Retrieved May 10, 2015 (http://www.forbes.com
/sites/ethansiegel/2015/04/10/finding-the-first-signs
-of-alien-life-and-why-nasa-thinks-its-coming-soon/).

INDEX

ABOUT THE AUTHOR

Carol Hand has a Ph.D. in zoology with a specialization in marine ecology. She has taught college biology, worked for standardized testing companies, developed multimedia science and technology curricula (including titles on life science and astronomy), and written more than twenty-five science and technology books for young people. She follows space exploration closely and, as a biologist, keenly anticipates the discovery of alien life.

PHOTO CREDITS

Cover, p. 1 Ron Miller/Stocktrek Images/Getty Images; pp. 4-5 ullstein bild/Getty Images; p. 9 iQoncept/Shutterstock.com; p. 12 BSIP/Universal Images Group/Getty Images; p. 14 Media for Medical/Universal Images Group/Getty Images; pp. 16-17 Georgie Holland/age fotostock/SuperStock; p. 19 Huntington Library/SuperStock; pp. 22, 33 NASA Ames/JPL-Caltech/T Pyle; p. 24 NASA Ames; p. 26 NASA/JPL-Caltech/MSSS; pp. 29, 53 NASA/JPL/University of Arizona; p. 31 NASA Ames/Jason Steffen, Fermilab Center for Particle Astrophysics; p. 35 Fotosearch/Archive Photos/Getty Images; pp. 36-37, 81, 82-83 NASA; p. 41 Michael Rougier/The LIFE Picture Collection/Getty Images; p. 43 Victor Bobbett/NASA; p. 44 Milton Wainwright; p. 46 © Justin Knight/EFE/ZUMA Press; p. 50 Media for Medical/Universal Images Group/Getty Images; p. 55 AFP/Getty Images; pp. 58-59 CfA/David Aguilar/NASA; p. 60 NASA/JPL/Space Science Institute; p. 63 Derek Lovley/Science Source; p. 66 James L Amos/Science Source/Getty Images; p. 69 Mike Agliolo/Science Source/Getty Images; p. 72 © AF archive/Alamy; pp. 78, 85 NASA/JPL-Caltech; p. 87 MIT; interior pages background images (space) Yuriy Kulik/Shutterstock.com, (light) Santiago Cornejo/Shutterstock.com; back cover Anatolii Vasilev/Shutterstock.com
Designer: Brian Garvey; Editor: Jacob Steinberg; Photo Researcher: Bruce Donnola